Mystic Meanderings

Philippa Drake

BookLeaf Publishing

India | USA | UK

Mystic Meanderings © 2024 Philippa Drake

All rights reserved.

No part of this publication may be reproduced, stored in a retrieval system, or transmitted, in any form or by any means, electronic, mechanical, photocopying, recording or otherwise, without the prior written permission of the presenters.

Philippa Drake asserts the moral right to be identified as author of this work.

Presentation by *BookLeaf Publishing*

Web: www.bookleafpub.com

E-mail: info@bookleafpub.com

ISBN: 9789360943233

First edition 2024

I would like to dedicate this book to my father Philip Drake who passed away suddenly on the 12th of September last year. One of the last things he said to me was to continue with my writing and music.

ACKNOWLEDGEMENT

I would like to thank Leanne McElhill for introducing me to BookLeaf Publishing on Facebook and a special thanks also to Tony and Heather Flood of Anderida Writers for supporting me in my writing endeavours and to Alistair Colley of Carbury Films who together with his late father Rod, created a fantastic website and a stunning film for me to promote my work.

PREFACE

My name is Philippa Drake and I would like to
present to you in verse my fantasy world of
sci-fi. Prepare to be moved, awed and dazzled
by the power of my digital quill at work.

Entwined in psychedelia

Twirling round electroid flares
deep in stars of psychedelia
the floral tribe murmur tenderly
and seraphic moons descend
to reveal divine mysteries
of ethereal kingdoms
lost in greyed out motion
where all is fettered
to a timeless continuum
of maelstrom.

Once upon a purple moon

Fallen lights
and purple moons
amid the stars
of untold gems
angel spun
and gilt entwined
honed in chords
of boundless joy
for mortal earth
to drift reposed.

In seraphic ecstasy

In seraphic union
we film our magic
beyond the ecstasy
of moonlight
and iridescent flares
as holograms dance
entwined fast in clouds
of deep mystery
honed by figures
transcending mortal visions.

Sunflower tears

Sonnenblumen are screaming
bloodied on rail tracks
Light oozes holy power
over the scrubland
where charred remnants exhale
a frosty rasp
and gaze in torpid wonder
at the tribe of spears.

Ghost images

5

Ghost images beam
fractal explosions
onto a canvas of AI greys
cloned in temporal war
as the roaring moon
spun fair Tournesol
into pixelated mesmer.

Obsidian worlds

In a nether world
I crown my head
with starless gauze
and wander barefoot
amid the sacred woodland tapestries
of vermeil webs
entwined around the domed
citadel mute and void
where crystalline figures
once reigned in stately visions
before the vaporous lord
devoured seraphic white.

Lamentations of an angel

Lo, the angel weeps
and bows to cast blood dew.
Stars eclipse at holy mourning
as light cracks bare fields of graves
where dim forms rise
to greet the Judge
with fond hope of clement words
that grant repose in sainted love.

Whispered moans

A red wizard prowls
in our holy sanctuary of light
bombarding flesh and bone
with acid laser beams.
Harken to the wailing
of our shadow figures
tremulant in terror
cored and propelled
to a paradise
where only carbon murmurs
amid the sunflower tribe
robed in poppy raiments.

Concentric circles

Into a vortex
of concentric circles
and iridescent holograms
I tumble adrift
propelled toward
greyed out light
pinioned by voices
of darkness
moaning in a fractured no man's land
where shards abound
in twisted smiles.

Captive to monochrome veils

Shadow forms entwine
beneath a carbon dome
of tremoring parasol gauze
that dances to the moon fire song.
Pink enters boldly and roars
devouring the splendour
of mages.

The grey cosplayer

When the grey phantom
of skeletal robes
pivots on stage
in macabre rhapsody
the grand hall mutes.
Figures bow, torpid
crystallised in a nanosecond
of void murmuring
bony enchantment
as the midnight hour descends
tearing kaleidoscopic visions
from the dreams of mortal man
who gazes forlorn at billowing
embers.

Zombie transmutations

A zombie hologram sparkles
with fanged haunting
of vapour crones
who stride in ember woods
forever tortured
as the dominion of blood
propels its grey armies
toward iridescent visions.

Noughts and crosses

Noughts and crosses in the air
branded by red artifice
of laser power
magnetised stridently
in networked turrets
pulsating a crazed melody of sonic
vibrations
where Mr Tinnitus commands
a mute yes, yes.

Shadows of projection

A boa coiled six heads
of blazing crimson
round wingèd maidens.
Retinues anointed for grace
treated with old monsters.
Exalted beings
moaned in shadows
of projection.

Child of many grooms

In the foetid swamp
of variegated circles
a babe moans
red and purple
tossed among fractured grooms
named Legion.
Wan is her bouquet
void of orange blossom
her gown, a carbon drape.

Transmuting iridescence

Stars rise eternal
in the tangle of numb hearts
and radiate haloed magic
transmuted iridescence
amid howling masters
dark angels of our time.

Caught in a diamond flare

Beneath a crimson moon
we paused to kiss
and pledge our vows
in the wingèd embrace
of holy amour
amid crystalline majesty
and ethereal powers.

Resplendent artifice

Vermillion beings entwine
and project wonders of transmutation
in the purpled gloaming.
By ardent sophistry
mortals bow to Meta tribes
and rack wingèd guardians.

Deceive, inveigle, obfuscate

Artful ruse propels myriads
to live dismemberment
in stentorian caverns
where the zeroed graft
brain and bone
onto a purpled circuitry
of dark awakening.

Auric imaginings

Amid the roar
of peripheral entities
and carbonised worlds
I dream of wingèd trance
honed by a sparkling muse
to guide monochrome visions
forlorn in the matrix.

The kerosine clock

21

Unworldly melodies play thrice.
Kerosine smoulders deep
within the towering rosewood clock.
Ochre flares; time detonates.
Past, present and future fragment
into billowing embers
to pass out of all reminiscence.

Dragons in the morn

In the silver of the morn
I gaze upon a dragon roar.
All booming red with dark power
He tears light before its birth.
Azure weeps blood; sun drips grey
In dryad realms the magic rots.

Pinioned

Pinioned to a web of chrome
awaiting the cudgel
hid deep in coiling miasmas
where unknown shadows
fracture and transmute
in a grisly time game
of infinite projections.

Towards mystic lands

Across the sea
to greet mauve light
where pearl rimmed stars
reign in harmony.

O perfect love
and wings of grace
surround the realm
in mystic song
before a glory child
of crowns.

By a dog rose tree
flayed red and shorn
I gaze upon the wondrous
prince divine.

In memoriam

Remember us
when we pass
into the wild
to meet grey.

On the steps
of a shorn earth
where crimson flows
bone dust fouls air
stars rain lead bolts
as fangs gore wings
of pearl and gold.

Remember us
Remember us
when we pass
when we pass.

An angel came to town

An angel came to town
with flame of face
and thunderous voice
to manifest his boundless tribe
in a world where souls are grey.

O wings of power
below fair stars
anoint and cover us
Rise holy mount
unite the red and purple lambs in chains

O hymns of peace and light
surround us
Grant the strength to stand for truth
when glory fails

An angel came to town
Strange tongues he spoke
to change the script of man
and lead him through eternity
transfixed by his heart.

Light the torch of truth

We will rise again
We will resurrect
No more as slaves
to the ghouls
of tyranny.

O light shine forth
O light conquer
the shadows
of fear and doubt.

Enfold us in your wings
holy angel choirs
guide all hearts swift
with an almighty flame.

Perpetual suppuration

Black roses
thorn imprinted
graze a fevered brow.
Lacerations
of perpetual swords
macerate a heart
born of sunlit hues
when diamond beams
awoke in merry flight
to dance with angel doves
at the glory hour of song
on a smiling day.

The wingèd warrior

I wing to war
my heart pure Sith
a storm of fire
amid the blades
carved word fangs
gall inscribed.
When flames dim
ice crowns nail wounds
that feel no kiss
of time reposed.

Vaporiser of words

Crimson beings
hurtle to realms
and fire an EM wave.
Organic forms convulse
void of words and melody
cored bots adrift
in a zeroed web
of roaring diktats.

Slayer of emotions

When the phantom howls
fire in hearts erodes.
Ice numbs crystal tears
joy rots and fractures
in razor, carbon shards
Mortal man ebbs mute
as a hollow shade.

Song light

Commune
with the world
gloriously.
Step boldly
into your song light
amid the rasping
of gored wings
oozing crimson
in the docile majesty
of mauve skies

Empire of doom

Amid crowns of starlight
thunder roars to garrote
ancient melodies and choirs
who materialise on earth
to unveil sacred mysteries
of whirling, infinite dimensions
that menace the empire of skulls.

www.ingramcontent.com/pod-product-compliance
Lightning Source LLC
LaVergne TN
LVHW010929200726

843509LV00013B/2140